To Linny Avallone,

Building a Biblical Worldview Verse by Verse

Key Scriptures That Answer 52 Essential Worldview Questions

BRANNON HOWSE
President and Founder of Worldview Weekend

BUILDING A BIBLICAL WORLDVIEW VERSE BY VERSE
Published by Worldview Weekend Publishing
a division of Worldview Weekend

© 2007 by Brannon Howse
International Standard Book Number:
0-9785014-4-6

Cover Design by JoePotter.com
Page Design & Typesetting by TGamble Productions

Unless noted otherwise, Scripture quotations are from
The Holy Bible, New King James Version (NKJV)
© 1994 by Thomas Nelson, Inc.

FOR INFORMATION:
WWW.WORLDVIEWWEEKEND.COM

PRINTED IN THE UNITED STATES OF AMERICA

DEDICATION

This book is dedicated to my three children, Landon, Libby and Logan Howse. May you hide God's Word in your heart that you might not sin against Him.

Love,

Dad

September 18, 2007

ACKNOWLEDGMENTS

Thank you to my editor Greg Webster, to Steve Gamble and Bob Heyer of TGamble Productions for page layout, and to Joe Potter for cover design.

ENDORSEMENT

"As parents of six young children, Chelsea and I have put teaching our kids a solid, Christian worldview at the top on our priority list. *Building a Biblical Worldview Verse by Verse* by Brannon Howse is a great tool for dinner time devotions. We love it and you will too."

Kirk Cameron

TABLE OF CONTENTS

Contents

FOREWORD

Every parent should be committed to instilling in their children a Biblical worldview, but understand that this is not accomplished unless parents teach them sound Biblical doctrine. My wife and I were consistent in nightly family devotions, and we routinely taught doctrine by inculcating our children with the Word of God. The reward is that today our grown children are all actively serving the Lord and discipling our grandchildren as we discipled them.

Second Timothy 3:15 points out that by studying the Scriptures as a child Timothy was made wise unto salvation. You may want to use this book as a family devotional, but even more, I encourage you to use it as a resource by which you and your children memorize scripture.

Chuck Swindoll extols the necessity of scripture memorization:

> I know of no other single practice in the Christian life more rewarding, practically speaking, than memorizing Scripture....No other single exercise pays greater spiritual dividends! Your prayer life will be strengthened. Your witnessing will be sharper and much more effective. Your attitudes and outlook will begin to change. Your mind will become alert and observant. Your confidence and assurance will be enhanced. Your faith will be solidified.[1]

As a Christian parent or grandparent the long-term value of knowing Scripture by heart should give you a deep passion for the importance of memorizing scripture with your children or grandchildren. Psalm 119:9,11 makes this benefit clear:

"How can a young man cleanse his way? By taking heed according to Your word... Your word I have hidden in my heart, that I might not sin against You."

By memorizing scripture, your children will be able to respond quickly by quoting scripture when tempted to sin. As your children go through life, they will encounter all sorts of false worldviews vying for their hearts and minds, and it is in those times I believe the Holy Spirit will use these scriptures to convict and encourage them.

Finally, the Bible describes children as arrows you can send forth to battle for the cause of Christ. Imagine the extraordinary influence your child will have when he or she is able to answer questions from skeptics and critics by quoting scripture.

I commend this book to you, and I thank Brannon Howse for providing yet another excellent resource for Christians.

RAY COMFORT
September 2007

---

[1] Chuck Swindoll, *Growing Strong in the Seasons of Life* (Grand Rapids: Zondervan, 1994), p.61.

PREFACE

It has been said that necessity is the mother of invention, and that is certainly the reason this book is in print today. Like many that make up this series, it was written out of my own need as a father. The necessity to teach my children Biblical doctrine weighed heavily on me—not in spite of the fact that they were *only* 4, 7 and 10 when this book was written but *because* they were so young and in need of instruction from early on.

Hopefully, you think it's normal that a father would be so concerned about teaching Christian truths to children, but you would be shocked to find out how many parents, and even pastors and Sunday school teachers, do not think about teaching children anything but simplistic Bible stories. They ignore a child's need to know the truth behind the tales. The American church is in a sad state today because most have neglected doctrine in favor of entertaining stories.

I recognize from my own upbringing the astonishing shortcomings of my Christian school and church, and I have been committed to laying the foundation for my own children so they will not be false converts as was I until an adult.

To accomplish the goal of training my children, I turned several years ago to a catechism for children. The book was structured so as to ask a theological and doctrinal question. Then children were to memorize a long paragraph with huge words that most adults could not define. I found myself scratching out certain words and substituting others my children could understand. After a few family devotions with this book, I realized my children were not going to learn sound doctrine this way!

Since my family and I travel thousands of miles each year to one speaking engagement after another, I have lots of time to think as I sit behind the wheel of our motor coach. So one day I asked myself, "What do I want my kids to learn"? To that simple question I arrived at a simple answer: *I want my kids to learn how to think Biblically.* To do that, I knew they had to learn doctrine, and the best source for that is the Bible. After all, which would I rather have them commit to memory: a manmade paragraph or the divinely inspired word of God?

Later that day, I typed out 52 questions—one for the kids to work on each week of the year—on my laptop. They are the questions for which I want my children to have a ready answer, from memory, from the Word of God. After coming up with my 52 questions, I searched the Scriptures for just the right verse to quickly answer each question.

While I was writing this book, my then 10-year-old son was dreaming about the upcoming hunting season. He imagined owning a particular 20-gauge shotgun and joining me and my two labs for quail and pheasant hunting when he turned 11 early in the fall. Although my son had been saving his pennies, he counted out his jar of coins and bills only to discover he had nowhere near the funds needed to buy his gun.

I sensed a motivational opportunity, so once I completed this manuscript, I printed it out and placed it in a three-ring binder. I told him that if he could memorize all the verses and be ready to answer any of the 52 questions with the appropriate Bible verse, I would buy the shotgun for him. The challenge resonated with him, and within three days he had memorized the first five verses. He also mapped out a plan to memorize all the verses in time to go hunting.

Over the next few weeks I asked, "Who created the universe," and my son would quote John 1:3. "Why is there evil in the world?" He quoted 1 John 3:8. Each time I threw out one of the 52 doctrinal and worldview questions, he answered them with a Bible verse. *Wow. How cool,* I thought. *He's learning doctrine—and Scripture!*

My boy is now well on his way to memorizing all the verses, and I really can't wait to buy him that shotgun. He'll make a great hunting partner. And if the Lord tarries and my son has a son, he can pass along that shotgun, together with the story of why his father bought it for him. The gun will be not only a great family heirloom but the physical symbol of a spiritual dynasty in the making. *Oh that his shotgun were passed down to 10 generations of Howse sons as a reward for hiding the Word of God in their hearts!*

Brannon Howse
August 2007

INTRODUCTION

From the Worldview Weekend platform, on my radio program, in several books, and through numerous articles, I've sounded the alarm about the sorry worldviews held by many evangelical Christians. Numerous studies—perhaps the most stunning of which was done by the Southern Baptist Church of its own youth—reveal that the lifestyles, values, and resulting worldviews of most of those that attend "evangelical churches" is no different from the world and that a large majority of students leave the church after graduating from high school, never to return.

While the studies reveal the problem, they don't explain what has caused it. But I believe I know. The root is that our churches are filled with false converts—a problem I identify with all too readily because, despite being raised in a Christian home, taught in a Christian school, and a member of a Bible-believing church, I was a false convert myself until becoming an adult. And the really scary part is that it's not all that hard to do!

I played the "game" (even though I didn't know I was playing a game) throughout my teen years. I thought I was saved because I believed in Jesus Christ, had prayed the "sinner's prayer," walked the aisle, and had been baptized. I was "sorry" for my sins, but it was not the kind of sorrow that produced repentance unto salvation.

My wake-up call came when I read the book of 1 John and recognized ten clear signs of a true convert but saw very few of those signs manifested in my own life. After searching the Scriptures further, I discovered the source of my dysfunctional attempt at Christianity in 2 Corinthians 7:9-10:

> Now I rejoice, not that you were made sorry, but that your sorrow led to repentance. For you were made sorry in a godly manner, that you might suffer loss from us in nothing. For godly sorrow produces repentance leading to salvation, not to be regretted; but the sorrow of the world produces death.

True repentance was missing from my heart and, hence, my life! "Godly sorrow" causes someone to turn and go in the opposite direction of a willfully sinful life. True repentance leads to a change in a person's life, priorities, and desires, and it produces God-honoring fruit.

You see, many people say they believe in Jesus, but this does not make them saved. Recall that the Bible says demons believe in Jesus (James 2:19) but so what? It's not a saving belief.

Too often people say they are saved because they are

sorry for the bad things they do, but they continue to will-fully practice sin (can you say "Sunday Christian"?). The 2 Corinthians passage makes clear that there is a worldly sorrow that leads to death and another, godly, sorrow that produces repentance leading to salvation.

What finally jolted me to realize I was not a good person, that I was totally depraved and deserved hell, was my encounter with the Biblical doctrine of the moral law—the Ten Commandments. I recognized that only a godly sorrow that leads to repentance and salvation would do. The moral law revealed my true condition—my extreme sinfulness and depravity.

Sadly, repentance is not a Christian doctrine we hear taught often enough (many churches *never* teach it) and the result? A church filled with false converts. This dire reality should concern all of us because Scripture is forth-right about how important this is:

- The word "repent" and its various forms are used over 100 times in the Bible.

- John the Baptist preached in the wilderness, "Repent, for the kingdom of heaven is at hand!" (Matthew 3:2).

- Jesus preached this same message of repentance. Mark 1:14, 15 says, "Now after John was put in prison, Jesus came to Galilee, preaching the gospel of the kingdom of God, and saying, 'The time is fulfilled, and the kingdom of God is at hand. Repent, and believe the gospel'."

- In Mark 6, Jesus sends out the 12 disciples two by two. Verse 12 states, "So they went out and preached that people should *repent*" (italics mine).

Every day 150,000 people step off into eternity and a frightening percentage of them fall into eternal judgment. I imagine that many who wind up under judgment are shocked when they grasp their situation. Many will have thought they lived a good life as defined by today's standards. They went to church, perhaps even walked the aisle and got baptized. Some even taught Sunday school. But Jesus warned this would happen:

> Not everyone who says to me, "Lord, Lord," will enter the kingdom of heaven, but the one who does the will of my Father who is in heaven. On that day many will say to me, "Lord, Lord, did we not prophesy in your name, and cast out demons in your name, and do many mighty works in your name?" And then will I declare to them, "I never knew you; depart from me, you workers of lawlessness." (Matthew 7:21-23)

Besides the all-important reason of keeping people from having to hear Jesus say "depart from me," there are 11 benefits here and now of teaching Biblical doctrine.

1. Biblical doctrine builds discernment and reveals the will of God for our lives.

• Discernment

What parent does not want their children to have discernment to make Godly decisions? Discernment and sound judgment are a by-products of teaching Biblical doctrine.

1 Thessalonians 5:21 says, "but test everything, hold fast what is good."

And Romans 12:2 commands, "Do not be conformed to this world, but be transformed by the renewal of your mind, that by testing you may discern what is the will of God, what is good and acceptable and perfect."

• Revealing the will of God for our lives

In John 7:17 Jesus said, "If anyone wills to do His will, he shall know concerning doctrine, whether it is from God or whether I speak on My own authority.

2. Biblical doctrine prepares us for every good work.

2 Timothy 3:16-17: "All Scripture is given by the inspiration of God, and is profitable for doctrine, for reproof, for correction, for instruction in righteousness, that the man of God may be complete, thoroughly equipped for every good work."

3. There has been a vast falling away from Biblical truth.

The Bible describes this great apostasy or this falling away from Biblical truth in 2 Timothy 4:3-4:

"For the time will come when they will not endure sound doctrine, but according to their own desires, because they have itching ears, they will heap up for themselves teachers; and they will turn their ear away from truth and be turned aside to fables."

4. False teaching is destroying lives.

Enemies of the truth know exactly how to encourage false teaching: *"Education is thus a most powerful ally of humanism. What can the theistic Sunday schools, meeting for an hour once a week, and teaching only a fraction of the children, do to stem the tide of a five-day program of humanistic teaching?"*

—1933, Charles Francis Potter, *Humanism: A New Religion*

And Colossians 2:8 prescribes the antidote: "Beware lest anyone cheat you through philosophy and empty deceit, according to the tradition of men, according to the basic principles of the world, and not according to Christ."

5. Biblical doctrine is not boring but a strong mooring.

As I said earlier, most self-professing Christians cannot articulate, much less defend, the essential doctrines of the Christian faith, but why is it that we spend so much time on things that will not last and that do not matter? Adults as well as teens can tell you all about pop culture, about sports teams and superstars but can these same teens and adults tell you how we know Jesus is God, how we know the Bible is true, or how we know Jesus rose from the dead?

Biblical doctrine is the Gospel, the will of God for our lives. It is what Jesus talked about during his earthly ministry. In spite of how it's sometimes been presented, the real picture of Jesus and His teachings is riveting. Jesus commanded respect, inspired commitment, and renewed lives in ruin.

6. Biblical doctrine taught early and consistently builds a faith that lasts.

In 2 Timothy 3:15 Paul, speaking about Timothy, says, "And that from childhood you have known the Holy Scriptures, which are able to make you wise for salvation through faith which is in Christ Jesus."

Who was it that taught Timothy the scriptures from such an early age? 2 Timothy 1:5 answers the question: "When I call to remembrance the genuine faith that is in you, which dwelt first in your grandmother Lois and your mother Eunice which I am persuaded is in you also."

Timothy's mother and grandmother taught him early, and he became one of the most powerful leaders in the first century church.

Deuteronomy 6:7 also reminds us to always be teaching God's truth to our children: "You shall teach them diligently to your children, and shall talk of them when you sit in your house, when you walk by the way, when you lie down, and when you rise up."

7. Biblical doctrine stirs the heart and mind.

"Heart" refers to the core of a person's being, and it is significant that the Bible mentions the heart 826 times.

Proverbs 4:23 explains that out of the *heart* "spring the issues of life."

From the heart proceed our good and bad thoughts, emotions, and behavior. So preparing the soil of a child's or teen's heart is crucial if we want to plant the seeds of Biblical truth and see them grow to maturity.

The Bible also commands us to love the Lord our God with all our *heart*, soul, strength, and *mind*. And Romans 10:10 makes the point: "For with the heart one believes unto righteousness, and with the mouth confession is made unto salvation."

8. Because there is no application without acquisition.

If we want to see our children, friends and family apply Biblical truth to all areas of life, they must first know what the truth is. Knowledge means the acquisition of truth; wisdom means the application of truth.

So where do we find knowledge and wisdom?

Proverbs 2: 6 explains, "For the Lord gives wisdom; from his mouth come knowledge and understanding"

Proverbs 9:10: "The fear of the Lord is the beginning of wisdom."

And Proverbs 1:7: "The fear of the Lord is the beginning of knowledge."

If adults and teens are to acquire wisdom and knowledge, we must encourage them to study Biblical doctrine and come to understand the character and nature of God it reveals.

9. Biblical doctrine convicts those that contradict.

Titus 1:9 says: "Holding fast the faithful word as he has been taught that he may be able, by sound doctrine, both to exhort and convict those who contradict." The scriptures are great at setting the record straight—whether in theology, doctrine, or lifestyle.

Remember, too, what 2 Timothy 3: 16 says: "All Scripture is given by inspiration of God, and is profitable for doctrine, for reproof, for correction, for instruction in righteousness."

10. Biblical doctrine will last forever.

The Bible says that grass withers and the flower fades but the Word of God stands forever. The reason is, as John 1:1 tells us, the Word of God *is* God: "In the beginning was the Word and the Word was with God and the Word was God."

So, when we commit ourselves to teaching and training hearts and minds with the Word of God, we are planting in the lives of others something that will last through all eternity.

11. Because lives are at stake, and it is appointed unto every man to die once and then face judgment.

Pay close attention to James 5:19-20: "Brethren, if any among you wanders from the truth, and someone turns him back, let him know that he who turns a sinner from the error of his way will save a soul from death and cover a multitude of sins."

Marching Orders

Would a fireman ignore a fire alarm, lean back in his recliner and watch the rest of the ballgame as hundreds of souls perish in a burning office building? Would an emergency room doctor sip coffee in the break room, reading the latest fishing magazine and ignore the Code Blue alert over the hospital P.A. system? Yet today, Christian school administrators, Sunday School teachers, youth pastors, senior pastors, Christian college professors and presidents, deacons, elders, and parents are just as culpable as they ignore the warnings, the cultural flashing lights, and all the social sirens that scream a spiritual Code Blue—the warning of imminent spiritual and eternal death.

Many of them won't be disturbed because they are busy entertaining and being entertained. They won't be distracted because they caught up giving adults and teens what they want, not what they need. They rally to be inclusive, not offensive. They're committed to consensus more than truth, customers over converts, donors over disciples, a big tent over the narrow way, and self-actualization over self-sacrifice. They will not be awakened from their malaise because they don't want to change their priorities or practice. The Christian life they falsely conjure offers everything and requires nothing.

Yet we should not be discouraged. God has seldom, if ever, moved among the majority, but He has historically and providentially worked among a remnant. And believe me, there is a remnant. It's thrilling to see how many and how strong they are who flock to Worldview Weekends because they know their need. As you read this book and share it with your children, you are part of that vestige of hope.

I thank God someone once spoke doctrine into my life, revealed the true condition of my heart and mind, and declared Code Blue for my soul. It's time we declare Code Blue for the American church and return to teaching sound Biblical doctrine before any more step unwittingly into eternity. I pray that this little book will be used by thousands of parents and grandparents to teach their children Christian doctrine. If we remain faithful to teaching a Biblical worldview and teaching sound theology, we will see lives saved for Christ.

Question 1:

WHO CREATED THE UNIVERSE?

Answer: John 1:3

"All things were made through Him, and without Him nothing was made that was made."

Further explanation:

When you look at a beautiful painting, you know it had a painter. When you look at a sculpture, you know it had a sculptor. When you look at a building, you know an architect designed it. However, when naturalists look at the world, they choose not to credit a designer with the feat. The mystifying order and complexity of the universe and its contents loudly proclaim a designer, and common sense dictates that the greater the design, the greater the designer. Historian and philosopher of science Stephen Meyer has said, "We have not yet encountered any good in principle reason to exclude design from science."[1]

William Paley went to Cambridge in 1759 to study mathematics. He later taught at Cambridge for nine years and was a great defender of Christianity. Paley argued that there must be only one Designer, since there is displayed in nature a uniformity of divine purpose in all parts of the world. [2]

Paley refined what is known as the teleological argument for the existence of God. The analysis begins by observing the design in the world and concludes that there is a designer beyond the world. Paley characterized the argument this way:

(1) Every watch has a watchmaker;

(2) The world is more complex than a watch;

(3) Hence, the world must have had a world maker.[3]

Question 2:

WHY IS THERE EVIL IN THE WORLD?

Answer: 1 John 3:8

*"He who sins is of the devil,
for the devil has sinned from the beginning.
For this purpose the Son of God was
manifested, that He might destroy
the works of the devil."*

Further explanation:

This is perhaps one of the most common questions of non-Christians. Often the skeptics and critics of Christianity will point to all the evil in the world and say this proves that God either does not exist or, if He does, He is not a loving God.

"God is not the author of confusion" (1 Corinthians 14:33), and thus neither is He the author of evil. James 1:13 says: "Let no one say when he is tempted, 'I am tempted by God'; for God cannot be tempted by evil, nor does He Himself tempt anyone."

Satan is the father of lies (John 8:44). Evil not only comes from Satan but from the heart of man (Mark 7:21; Matthew 15:19).

God created man with a free will, and thus man can choose to do good or to do evil. Ideas have consequences, and thus much of the evil in the world is due to man's rebellion against God and His moral law.

Ephesians 2:5 says, "even when we were dead in trespasses, [God] made us alive together with Christ...." God would be completely justified in allowing sin and evil to consume us, but He intervened and provides the way for us to have victory over sin, death, and the grave.

*Q*uestion 3:

FOR WHAT PRIMARY PURPOSE WAS MANKIND CREATED?

Answer: 1 Corinthians 10:31

*"Therefore, whether you eat or drink,
or whatever you do,
do all to the glory of God."*

Further explanation:

Our main goal in life is to bring honor and glory to God. This worldview is completely opposite to that of Secular Humanists, who deny the existence of God and thus have the life goal of serving self and seeking pleasure and entertainment.

The Humanist Manifesto I proclaims: "The quest for the good life is still the central task for mankind."

This worldview of seeking pleasure is called hedonism, and it is taught and encouraged in many of our nation's public schools through values clarification courses. William Bennett, U.S. Secretary of Education under Ronald Reagan, has spoken out strongly against values clarification. Bennett reveals the dangers and consequences of the relativistic philosophies on which such curricula are based:

> People are bundles of wants; the world is a battlefield of conflicting wants; and no one has room for goodness, decency, or the capacity for a positive exercise of will. Moral maturity is certainly not to be found in the clarification of values, which is cast solely in the language of narrow self-gratification and is devoid of any considerations of decency whatsoever. Finally and ironically, Simon's approach emphatically indoctrinates—by encouraging and

even exhorting the student to narcissistic self-gratification.[4]

Christians must reject the humanistic worldview of hedonism and make the goal of their lives to glorify their Father who is in heaven, for this is the primary reason we were created.

Question 4:

WHO IS GOD?

Answer: John 4:24

"God is Spirit,
and those who worship Him
must worship in spirit and truth."

Further explanation:

God is a spirit, which means He is invisible. Colossians 1:15 says, "He [Jesus Christ] is the image of the invisible God.... "

1 Timothy 1:17 says, "Now to the King eternal, immortal, invisible...."

When John says we must worship God in spirit, this is not a reference to the Holy Spirit but to our spirit, heart, or soul. Many Christians think that in order to worship God they must be involved in certain external activities, practices, or rituals. However, John says true worship occurs when our hearts are focused on truth or on the Word of God, which is a reflection of the character and nature of God.

John 14:6 says that Jesus Christ is the way, the truth, and the life. Truth is not a "what" but a "who," and truth is revealed through the study of God's Word. John 1:1 says that in the beginning was the Word, and the Word was with God, and the Word was God.

So let's review: God is a Spirit, and if we want to worship God we must study the Scriptures, where the truth or the character and nature of God are revealed. By studying and conforming our hearts and spirits to the character and nature of God, we can encounter true fellowship, communion, or worship of God.

Question 5:

IS THERE MORE THAN ONE GOD?

Answer: Isaiah 45:5-6

*"I am the Lord; there is no other God.
I have prepared you, even though you do not
know me, so all the world from east to west
will know there is no other God.
I am the Lord, and there is no other."*

Further explanation:

There is only one God, and this God exists as three Persons: the Father, the Son (Jesus Christ), and the Holy Spirit. Jesus' final words in the book of Matthew are, "Go therefore and make disciples of all the nations, baptizing them in the name of the Father and of the Son and of the Holy Spirit..." (Matthew 28:19).

In John 1:14 we learn that "the Word became flesh and dwelt among us, and we beheld His glory, the glory as of the only begotten of the Father, full of grace and truth." Jesus consistently referred to God as His Father, praying to Him and teaching His disciples to pray to Him as well. When Jesus was baptized by John in the Jordan, the voice of God "came from heaven, 'You are My beloved Son, in whom I am well pleased'" (Mark 1:11).

Jesus told his followers, "And I will pray the Father, and He will give you another Helper, that He may abide with you forever—the Spirit of truth, whom the world cannot receive, because it neither sees Him nor knows Him; but you know Him, for He dwells with you and will be in you" (John 14:16-17). The Old Testament reveals that the Holy Spirit was present and active at Creation (Genesis 1:2) and has always been, but it is the New Testament that shows us His divine personhood more clearly, especially when Jesus was baptized by John and in the second chapter of Acts, on the Day of Pentecost.

Question 6:

WHAT IS SIN?

Answer: 1 John 3:4

*"Whoever commits sin
also commits lawlessness,
and sin is lawlessness."*

Further explanation:

Sin is what offends God or what is contrary to His character and nature and revealed through the moral law. Thus, sin is breaking the moral law or the Ten Commandments.

We must not be afraid to use the word "sin." "All unrighteousness is sin..." (1 John 5:17). According to the book of Romans, the moral law is written on the heart and mind of every person—the conscience ("con" means with and "science" means knowledge). Because of the conscience, every time people sin or rebel against God, they know it is wrong. Romans 7:7 assures us that the law convicts people of their sin. And "...to him who knows to do good and does not do it, to him it is sin" (James 4:17).

Romans 1:21 reminds us, "although they knew God, they did not glorify Him as God, nor were thankful, but became futile in their thoughts, and their foolish hearts were darkened." And Romans 2:15 points out that people "show the work of the law written in their hearts, their conscience also bearing witness, and between themselves their thoughts accusing or else excusing them."

People can either accept the guilty feeling of the law that accuses them of their transgression when they sin, or they can excuse the guilty feeling and learn to ignore it. If people ignore the guilt long enough or often enough, they will become liars whose "consciences are seared with a hot iron" (1 Timothy 4:2).

Question 7:

WHO HAS SINNED?

Answer: Romans 3:23

"[F]or all have sinned and fall short of the glory of God."

Further explanation:

Everyone has broken the law. No one can claim to warrant entry into heaven because they have "lived a good enough life." God's standard is that people must keep the complete moral law, and no one has done that. The purpose of the law is not to save us. It is to condemn us, to show us our true state, to reveal our sin, and to show us we deserve God's wrath.

Romans 3:20 explains that the purpose of the law is to get people to stop trying to justify their sin. And Romans 3:10 explains, "There is none righteous, no, not one." The Preacher tells us in Ecclesiastes 7:20, "For there is not a just man on earth who does good and does not sin."

"If we say that we have no sin, we deceive ourselves, and the truth is not in us" (1 John 1:8). No one has kept all the Ten Commandments except Jesus Christ. If someone ever claims he or she has not sinned, simply ask if he or she has ever told a lie, stolen something, taken the Lord's name in vain, or wanted something that someone else owns.

Anyone who is honest will have to admit to breaking every one of these commandments. Besides, people who are not honest in admitting they have broken these commandments are lying—which means they have broken the Ninth Commandment.

Question 8:

WHAT IS THE PURPOSE OF THE MORAL LAW OR THE TEN COMMANDMENTS?

Answer: Romans 7:7

*"What shall we say then?
Is the law sin? Certainly not!
On the contrary, I would not have known
sin except through the law."*

Further explanation:

The purpose of the moral law— Ten Commandments—is to reveal man's sinfulness and need for salvation. Salvation is granted to those who place their faith in the risen Jesus Christ and repent of their sins. In Galatians 3:24, Paul tells us that the law is the tutor to bring us to Christ.

The Ten Commandments also teach us our duty to God (1-4) and our duty to our fellow men (5-10). Jesus said, "You shall love the Lord your God with all your heart, with all your soul, and with all your mind. This is the first and great commandment. And the second is like it: 'You shall love your neighbor as yourself.' On these two commandments hang all the Law and the Prophets" (Matthew 22:37-39).

The great preacher John Wesley said that we need to preach 90% law and 10% grace. Ray Comfort, in his presentation, "Hell's Best Kept Secret," explains that when we use the moral law in our churches and evangelism efforts, we create converts who:

- understand the reason for God's wrath
- understand God's grace and mercy
- understand their sinful condition
- have gratitude to God for salvation
- understand they don't deserve the hope of heaven based on their own merit
- have gratitude that creates zeal for sharing the moral law with the lost.[5]

Question 9:

CAN A PERSON BE SAVED BY KEEPING THE TEN COMMANDMENTS OR THE MORAL LAW?

Answer: Galatians 2:21

"I do not set aside the grace of God; for if righteousness comes through the law, then Christ died in vain."

Further explanation:

If we could keep the moral law or the Ten Commandments, then Jesus Christ would not have had to come to earth and die for our sins. No one but Jesus has kept all the Commandments. James 2:10 explains that if we break even one of the commandments, we have broken them all: "For whoever shall keep the whole law, and yet stumble in one point, he is guilty of all."

Paul said, "Therefore, just as through one man sin entered the world, and death through sin, and thus death spread to all men, because all sinned" (Romans 5:12). And later, "Therefore, as through one man's offense judgment came to all men, resulting in condemnation, even so through one Man's righteous act the free gift came to all men, resulting in justification of life" (Romans 5:18).

Question 10:

WHY WAS JESUS CHRIST WILLING TO DIE FOR US?

Answer: Romans 5:8

"But God demonstrates His own love toward us, in that while we were still sinners, Christ died for us."

Further explanation:

Romans 5:9 tells us what we really deserve and why we should be so very grateful for God's love, mercy, and grace: "Much more then, having now been justified by His blood, we shall be saved from wrath through Him."

Jesus Christ died for us because He loves us and wants to save us from what we really deserve for our sins——God's wrath. We deserve His wrath because we have broken the moral law. We have offended a Holy God.

This is truly amazing grace. While we were yet enemies of God (sinners) Jesus Christ died for you and for me. I know I would give my life for any of my three kids or my wife, but would I be willing to give my life to save someone who hated me, who offended me over and over, or continually treated me with disrespect and disdain? That answer is a resounding "no"! Yet, that is exactly what Jesus did for the fallen, sinful race of man.

The words of Isaac Watts' classic hymn, "When I Survey the Wondrous Cross," fit well with Romans 5:8-9:

> See, from His head, His hands, His feet,
>> Sorrow and love flow mingled down:
> Did e'er such love and sorrow meet,
>> Or thorns compose so rich a crown?
> Were the whole realm of nature mine,
>> That were a present far too small;
> Love so amazing, so divine,
>> Demands my soul, my life, my all.

Question 11:

WHAT DOES EVERY PERSON DESERVE FOR HIS OR HER SINS?

Answer: Romans 6:21

*"What fruit did you have then
in the things of which you are now ashamed?
For the end of those things is death."*

Further explanation:

The word "fruit" in this verse means benefit. In other words, what benefit did we have or what did we gain for the sin for which we are now ashamed and which was leading us to death?

Each and every one of us deserves spiritual death or eternity in hell for our sins. Romans 6:23 tells us that the wages of sin or the price of sin is death.

Question 12:

WHAT IS THE RESULT OF GODLY SORROW?

Answer: 2 Corinthians 7:10

"For godly sorrow produces repentance leading to salvation, not to be regretted; but the sorrow of the world produces death."

Further explanation:

Godly sorrow produces repentance. To repent means to turn from sin and to stop practicing sin as a lifestyle. This does not mean a person will never sin again, but there is a big difference between stumbling into sin and intentionally diving in.

A repentant heart is born out of a person's awareness of his or her deep-seated sinfulness and the understanding that everyone deserves the wrath of God. A repentant person who surrenders his or her life to Christ receives eternal life with Christ. Eternal life is ours at the moment of salvation because Christ fully paid for sin by dying in place of sinners. 2 Corinthians 7:9-10 says:

> Now I rejoice, not that you were made sorry, but that your sorrow led to repentance. For you were made sorry in a godly manner, that you might suffer loss from us in nothing. For godly sorrow produces repentance leading to salvation, not to be regretted; but the sorrow of the world produces death.

True repentance is a Godly sorrow for sin. It is turning and going in the opposite direction of a willfully sinful lifestyle. True repentance leads to a change in a person's life as he or she grows in relationship with Jesus Christ.

Question 13:

WHAT ROLES DO THE HEART AND MIND PLAY IN SALVATION?

Answer: Romans 10:10

"For with the heart one believes unto righteousness, and with the mouth confession is made unto salvation."

Further explanation:

The Bible mentions the heart 826 times. "Heart" refers to the core of a person's being. Proverbs 4:23 says the heart is the source of life. From the heart proceed our good and bad thoughts, emotions, and behavior.

Your heart and mind comprise your soul, the core of who you are—and who you will still be after you die. The heart and mind will live forever and be judged by God (Romans 2:5; Revelation 2:23). The person who repents of sin and surrenders his or her will to the Lordship of Jesus Christ is the person who receives mercy and grace. That person has been saved by God on the basis of Christ's complete payment for sin at Calvary. In the day of destruction, the saved person is not judged for his or her sins.

The Bible says we are to love the Lord our God with all our *heart*, soul, strength, and *mind*. Unfortunately, many Christians ignore this last point. Christianity is not something we believe by blind faith. There are solid reasons to become a Christian. Scripture variously commands us to think, reason, discern, judge, determine, contend, and argue—all activities of the mind. Using one's mind in service to Jesus Christ is an act of worship and love.

In Scripture, the words "heart" and "mind" are often interchangeable, and at other times they complement one another. Jeremiah 17:9, for instance, describes the heart as "deceitful above all things, and desperately wicked," so the mind must moderate the heart.

Question 14:

WHEN JESUS SENT OUT THE DISCIPLES TWO BY TWO WHAT DID THEY DO?

Answer: Mark 6:12

*"So they went out and preached
that people should repent."*

Further explanation:

My friend Mark Cahill, who speaks for the Worldview Weekend, wrote an outstanding book entitled *One Thing You Can't Do in Heaven*. He offers a superb explanation of the real meaning and result of repentance:

> One topic that I believe we must talk about when we discuss sin is repentance. It seems to be a word that we don't use much in witnessing, and a word that some people don't want to use at all. Yet the word "repent" and its various forms is used over one hundred times in the Bible. It must be a very important word then, and something that we must understand.
>
> John the Baptist preached in the wilderness, "Repent, for the kingdom of heaven is at hand!" (Matthew 3:2).
>
> Jesus preached this same message of repentance. Mark 1:14, 15 says, "Now after John was put in prison, Jesus came to Galilee, preaching the gospel of the kingdom of God, and saying, 'The time is fulfilled, and the kingdom of God is at hand. Repent, and believe the gospel.'"
>
> In Mark 6, Jesus sends out the twelve disciples two by two. Verse 12 states, "So they went out and preached that people should repent." If Jesus sent

the disciples out preaching that people must repent of their sins, we ought to do the same.

Repentance is not when we feel bad because we got caught doing something wrong. True repentance is when we change our mind about our sin so our actions will not continue to be the same.[6]

Question 15:

WHAT IS THE FEAR OF THE LORD?

Answer: Proverbs 1:7

"The fear of the Lord is the beginning of knowledge."

Further explanation:

The book of Proverbs mentions the fear of the Lord numerous times. To fear the Lord is to have respect and reverence for God to the point that it causes our attitude, desires, will, and goals to reflect His character and nature. When we come to understand the character and nature of God we cannot help but have respect and reverence for Him.

The more we understand God's holiness, the more we realize how deprived and sinful we are and how much we deserve His wrath and judgment. God's amazing grace and mercy should cause any true believer to stand in awe and reverence before the King of Kings and Lord of Lords, who loves us and saved us from our sins.

Proverbs 8:13 points out, "The fear of the Lord is to hate evil." And Proverbs 9:10 explains, "The fear of the Lord is the beginning of wisdom."

Knowledge is the acquisition of truth, and wisdom is the application of truth. Everything that is consistent with the character and nature of God is true, and everything that is contrary to the character and nature of God is a lie. The more we study God's Word, His character and nature, the more we will fear the Lord; and the more we fear the Lord, the more knowledge and wisdom we acquire.

Question 16:

What does the Bible say about the person who does not believe in God?

Answer: Psalm 14:1

"The fool has said in his heart, 'There is no God.'"

Further explanation:

God is truth, and those who reject truth face two fairly dismal prospects. There's a spicy passage in Romans 1:20-22 that explains this:

> For since the creation of the world His invisible attributes arc clearly seen, being understood by the things that are made, even His eternal power and Godhead, so that they are without excuse, because, although they knew God, they did not glorify Him as God, nor were thankful, but became futile in their thoughts, and their foolish hearts were darkened. Professing to be wise, they became fools....

The dismal eternal prospect is this: When judgment day comes, there will be no excuse for not having known God.

The second consequence is more immediate: No matter how intellectually elite or culturally sophisticated the proponent of a non-God belief system may sound, people who reject God will become foolish—they'll "look stupid." The Greek word rendered "fools," literally means to "become stupid, worthless or purposeless."

With this in mind, perhaps you can better understand why far-left thinkers—professorial, student, or otherwise—sometimes sound so crazy. They cannot help but believe illogical things—about origins, social issues, moral values, or philosophy—because their prideful rejection of God has insulated them from considering the truth. As a result, God allows them the freedom to believe what is false and to go through the mental contortions necessary to create a system of thought that ignores Him.

Question 17:

WHY IS IT IMPORTANT TO THINK BIBLICALLY?

Answer: Proverbs 23:7

"For as he thinks in his heart,
so is he."

Further explanation:

The Bible tells us in Romans 12:2 not to be conformed to this world, but to be transformed by the renewing of our minds. Unfortunately, many self-professing Christians think Biblically in some ways but like a liberal or a Secular Humanist in others. Our Christian calling, though, is to bring *every* thought captive to the obedience of Jesus Christ.

The Bible is a reflection of the character and nature of God, and we can have a decidedly Biblical worldview on the issues of our day by "studying to show ourselves approved." In 2 Timothy 2:15 this direction is affirmed: "Be diligent to present yourself approved to God, a worker who does not need to be ashamed, rightly dividing the word of truth." Having command of a Biblical worldview does not come easily. It requires work—and requires the worker to study.

A worldview is the foundation of your values. Values determine how you act and how you live your life. Another way to describe a worldview is that it is a collection of your beliefs which make a difference in how you live. Everyone has a worldview. You are surrounded by friends, other students, teachers, and even family members that have their own ways of looking at things. Some of them have views that are different from Christianity. Various worldviews compete for your heart and mind, but unless a worldview lines up with the Bible, it won't give you a real picture of how things are.

Question 18:

WHERE DID THE SCRIPTURES COME FROM, AND FOR WHAT DO THEY PREPARE US?

Answer: 2 Timothy 3:16-17

"All Scripture is given by inspiration of God, and is profitable for doctrine for reproof, for correction, for instruction in righteousness, that the man of God may be complete, thoroughly equipped for every good work."

Further explanation:

We find in Scripture the doctrine—the teachings—of the Christian faith. To ignore doctrine is to ignore God's commandments, the teachings of Jesus Christ, and what the Bible reveals concerning salvation.

Biblical doctrine brings discernment. In order for children to understand God, we must teach them the moral law, because it is a reflection of God's character and nature. Everything consistent with the character and nature of God is truth, and everything contrary is untruth. True discernment comes from knowing the difference.

The author of the letter to the Hebrews said, "For though by this time you ought to be teachers, you need someone to teach you again the first principles of the oracles of God; and you have come to need milk and not solid food. For everyone who partakes only of milk is unskilled in the word of righteousness, for he is a babe. But solid food belongs to those who are of full age, that is, those who by reason of use have their senses exercised to discern both good and evil (Hebrews 5:12-14)."

Biblical doctrine also shows us God's will for our lives. In John 7:17 Jesus Himself says, "If anyone wills to do His (God's) will, he shall know concerning the doctrine, whether it is from God or whether I speak on My own authority."

Biblical doctrine addresses every major issue, whether it is, law, science, economics, history, family, social issues, religion, or education, and a Biblical worldview prepares us for every good work in any of these realms.

Question 19:

WHAT THREE NOUNS CAN BE ASCRIBED TO JESUS CHRIST?

Answer: John 14:6

"Jesus said to him, 'I am the way, the truth, and the life. No one comes to the Father except through Me.'"

Further explanation:

Jesus Christ made the most politically incorrect statement of all time when He said, "No one comes to the Father except through Me." Yes, He meant that following, serving, and believing in Buddha, Krishna, Mohammed, or any other spiritual leader would not bring eternal life. Any attempt to gain salvation or reach heaven apart from Him is futile—a message branded as "intolerant" in today's world. Liberals find this offensive largely because it means their definitions of truth are wrong.

Those who maintain a genuine desire to discover truth, though, will eventually find it. Josh McDowell, for example, set out to disprove Christianity and became one of the world's greatest Christian thinkers and defenders. In his book *Beyond Belief to Convictions*, he points out that truth is not just an abstract philosophical concept. Truth is a Person, namely, Jesus Christ.

As Josh says, "When we are careful to keep truth within that personal, relational context, it can change everything in the minds and hearts of our young people and the whole postmodern generation!"[7]

This shift from "what" to "Who" mandates a change in how we think of Christianity. Relating to or obeying moral and spiritual truth should not be thought of as a response to philosophical concepts, but rather as how we relate to a Person.[8]

Question 20:

WHY IS THE RESURRECTION OF JESUS CHRIST SO IMPORTANT?

Answer: 1 Corinthians 15:17

"And if Christ is not risen, your faith is futile; you are still in your sins!"

Further explanation:

All of Christianity hinges on the resurrection of Jesus Christ from the grave. If Jesus did not rise from the dead, then sin and the grave are not defeated. A savior that cannot save himself cannot save us. It is imperative that Christians be prepared to defend the overwhelming evidence that Jesus Christ rose from the dead and is the sinless Savior.

Many of Jesus' disciples were martyred in terrible ways: beheading, burning, dragging, beating, spearing, hanging, stoning, and crucifixion. Would these men have died for something they knew to be a lie or a trick they had played by stealing the body of Jesus? Even if one or two were determined to "stick to their story," it is not reasonable to think all of them would have died rather than admitting to the lie. The obvious conclusion is that the eyewitnesses to Jesus' resurrection told what they believed to be true and refused to change their story, even in the face of terrible persecution, torture, and death. As author Tim LaHaye puts it, "They signed their testimony in blood."[9]

They loved their Lord more than life and fully believed in what they had seen. They knew He had died for them, and now they were willing to die in order to proclaim Jesus as the sinless, risen Savior of the world.

*Q*uestion *21:*

WHAT HAPPENS TO THE PERSON WHO REJECTS GOD OVER AND OVER?

Answer: 2 Thessalonians 2:10-12

"and with all unrighteous deception among those who perish, because they did not receive the love of the truth, that they might be saved. And for this reason God will send them strong delusion, that they should believe the lie, that they all may be condemned who did not believe the truth but had pleasure in unrighteousness."

Further explanation:

Because God is truth, when people reject truth, they are rejecting God. They cannot claim they do not know truth because God has created every man and woman to know He exists. "For the wrath of God is revealed from heaven against all ungodliness and unrighteousness of men, who suppress the truth in unrighteousness, because what may be known of God is manifest in them, for God has shown it to them" (Romans 1:18-19).

If people continue to reject God over and over, God will eventually give them over to the lie, and they will not be able to tell right from wrong. Romans 2:15 speaks of the Gentiles, "who show the work of the law written in their hearts, their consciences also bearing witness, and between themselves and their thoughts accusing or else excusing them...." This verse explains that people can either accept the guilty feeling of the law, accusing them of their transgression when they sin, or they can simply excuse the guilty feeling and learn to ignore it. If people ignore the guilt and suppress the truth long enough or often enough, they will become liars whose consciences are seared (1 Timothy 4:2).

We can ignore God—even deny God—but because God has made Himself known by creating us in His image and by placing an understanding of His character and nature in the heart of every human being, no one will have an excuse at judgment for rejecting God and following the lie of humanism (Romans 1:20).

Question 22:

WHAT SHOULD CHRISTIANS BE PREPARED TO DO WHEN ASKED ABOUT THEIR FAITH IN JESUS CHRIST?

Answer: 1 Peter 3:15

"But sanctify the Lord God in your hearts, and always be ready to give a defense to everyone who asks you a reason for the hope that is in you, with meekness and fear...."

Further explanation:

We've already mentioned the transformation that took place when Josh McDowell set out to disprove Christianity. Yet his is not the only story of its kind. Former atheist Dr. Frank Harber studied nine of the world's major religions, trying to find out which one, if any, had a corner on the truth. At the end of his rigorous investigation, Harber concluded that Christianity is the one. Today, he holds a Ph.D. from Southwestern Seminary, which he earned faster than anyone in that institution's history. He is also one of America's premiere defenders of the Christian faith as an author, conference speaker, pastor of a church of more than 4,000, and host of a daily radio broadcast heard on more than 550 stations.

How did these two men conclude Christianity is true? They each determined that its essential doctrines can be confirmed. Worldview Weekend often receives feedback from people who were skeptics until they attended one of our conferences, read one of my books, or read the articles on our website. The Word of God is powerful and has promised not to return void. All we have to do is to be faithful in contending for the faith and leave the results to the Holy Spirit.

Question 23:

A LARGE GROUP OF PEOPLE SAW JESUS AFTER HE ROSE FROM THE DEAD. HOW MANY WERE IN THAT CROWD?

Answer: 1 Corinthians 15:6

"After that He was seen by over five hundred brethren at once, of whom the greater part remain to the present, but some have fallen asleep."

Further explanation:

Perhaps the greatest evidence for the resurrection of Jesus Christ is that more than *five hundred* eyewitnesses saw Him. And Jesus not only appeared to His followers but to one of the first century's greatest enemies of Christianity, Saul of Tarsus.

Saul was a Jewish leader who was responsible for killing numerous Christians because of their faith. Yet when Jesus, after His resurrection, appeared to Saul on the Damascus road, Saul was transformed and became one of the all-time greatest defenders of Christianity. In Acts 26:4-5, 9-23 Saul gives his testimony.

It is a fact of history that Saul of Tarsus was a leader of his day who persecuted Christians. It is also true that Saul changed radically, became known as Paul, and was a pivotal leader of the early church. So what would cause a man to change from hating, persecuting, and killing Christians to becoming a Christian and a defender of Christianity? Paul's own answer is the most logical conclusion—an encounter with the risen Lord.

In 1 Corinthians 15:6, Paul directs skeptics or critics to ask the eyewitnesses who had seen the resurrected Christ. Those who saw Jesus were changed and became willing to die rather than to say they had not seen Him alive after His crucifixion. Those who did die for their faith would have only had to say, "Jesus really is dead," and they could have lived. The disciples and eyewitnesses spoke the truth and refused to change their story in the face of persecution, torture, and death.

Question 24:

WHAT DOES THE BIBLE SAY ABOUT SELF-DEFENSE?

Answer: Exodus 22:2

"If the thief is found breaking in, and he is struck so that he dies, there shall be no guilt for his bloodshed."

Further explanation:

God allows for killing another human being only in the cases of self-defense and capital punishment. And in Genesis 9:6 the responsibility for bringing justice to a victim of murder is given specifically to the assailant's fellow human beings: "Whoever sheds man's blood, by man his blood shall be shed; for in the image of God He made man."

Question 25:

WHAT IS THE PURPOSE OF CIVIL GOVERNMENT?

Answer: 1 Peter 2:13-14

"Therefore submit yourselves to every ordinance of man for the Lord's sake, whether to the king as supreme, or to governors, as to those who are sent by him for the punishment of evildoers and for the praise of those who do good."

Further explanation:

These verses make clear that God's plan for civil government is to punish evildoers and to protect and praise those who do right. When civil government steps outside of God's ordained purpose and persecutes righteous people, promotes evil, or does injustice to the innocent, the moral authority of the civil government has been lost, and Christians are free to disobey.

Scripture calls rulers "ministers of God," which shows clearly how important the responsibility of a civic leader actually is. Since these leaders are ministers, it stands to reason that God would call Christians into this occupation just as He calls some people into the ministry of being a full-time pastor.

While God allows governments to come into being, that does not mean God approves of every government. According to Christ, the government should work in harmony with the church (Matthew 22:21), and when it does, God approves of the government in power.

While it is true that the church often flourishes during times of extreme persecution, this happens largely because of the civil disobedience of Christians who worship underground, smuggle Bibles, and distribute Scripture—contrary to the laws governing them. Disobedience to government may be required in the process of opposing evil, promoting righteousness, defending the weak, and providing for the safety of a person's family.

Question 26:

WHAT DOES THE BIBLE SAY ABOUT CIVIL DISOBEDIENCE?

Answer: Acts 5:29

"But Peter and the other apostles answered and said: 'We ought to obey God rather than men.'"

Further explanation:

Many Christians become uneasy about the subject of "civil disobedience" and invoke Romans 13 to avoid the responsibility of standing up to a deviant government. While it is crucial that Christians pursue civil disobedience only when obeying government requires us to *disobey* God, Scripture offers clear direction on when such action is acceptable. Kerby Anderson points out the following Biblical principles for civil disobedience:

1. The law or injunction being resisted should clearly be unjust and unbiblical.
2. The means of redress should be exhausted.
3. Christians must be willing to accept the penalty for breaking the law.
4. Civil disobedience should be carried out in love and with humility.
5. Civil disobedience should be considered only when there is some possibility of success.[10]

The interesting thing about Acts 5 is that God Himself sends an angel to release the apostles from jail and then has the angel specifically instruct them to go and continue in civil disobedience—in this instance, preaching the gospel in the temple, against the ruling of local authorities.

While you can hope that you never have to disobey the laws of your community, state, or country in order to walk in good conscience with God, there is no guarantee you'll never be called to civil disobedience. Knowing where you stand from a Biblical viewpoint, though, is the first step in being prepared to do whatever God requires.

Question 27:

WHAT DOES THE BIBLE SAY ABOUT THE IMPORTANCE OF ELECTING GODLY LEADERS?

Answer: Proverbs 29:2

"When the righteous are in authority, the people rejoice; but when a wicked man rules, the people groan."

Further explanation:

If our nation rejects God's authority, we will be allowing ourselves to accept the only alternative, which is "man"—and the resulting government—as the ultimate authority.

The Declaration of Independence states that "all men are created equal" and that "they are endowed by their Creator with certain unalienable rights." Our government should base its actions on whether or not they fulfill the purpose for which government was created—to protect our God-given rights. According to the Declaration, "to secure these rights, governments are instituted among men."

Benjamin Franklin contended, "Only a virtuous people are capable of freedom. As nations become corrupt and vicious, they have more need of masters."

In 1854 the U.S. House Judiciary Committee wrote: "Laws will not have permanence or power without the sanction of religious sentiment and without a firm belief that there is a Power above us that will reward our virtues and punish our vices."

If our leaders don't understand they will be held accountable in this life and the next to a Deity above our governments, there is no accountability to rule with justice and mercy, to defend the righteous, and to punish the wicked. History has proven this point well. Hitler, Stalin, Mussolini, and countless other tyrants who were professing (or de facto) atheists became our world's greatest mass murderers. In their atheistic worldviews, they were the highest authority. The twentieth century, the most murderous of any century in history, saw the deaths of 135 million people at the hands of Communists, according to the *Congressional Record*.[11]

Question 28:

WHAT DOES THE BIBLE SAY CONCERNING A NATION'S LAWS?

Answer: Proverbs 14:34

"Righteousness exalts a nation, but sin is a reproach to any people."

Further explanation:

Why did the Founders decide that America's laws were to be based on God's laws? Because they believed God's moral law was written on the hearts of all people. In his book *Original Intent*, David Barton points out, "The Founders believed the Bible to be the perfect example of moral legislation and the source of what they called 'the moral law'."

The Bible offers numerous verses that relate morality to government. Scripture calls all nations to promote righteousness—right living and justice:

- Righteousness exalts a nation, but sin is a reproach to any people (Proverbs 14:34).
- By the blessing of the upright the city is exalted, but it is overthrown by the mouth of the wicked (Proverbs 11:11).
- When the righteous are in authority, the people rejoice but when a wicked man rules, the people groan (Proverbs 29:2).
- Blessed are those who hunger and thirst for righteousness, for they shall be filled (Matthew 5:6).

So "legislating morality" is not a violation of any standard, principle, or proper philosophy of government. Moral purpose lies behind every law. Despite the beliefs of many misguided individuals, Christians must be involved in the legislative process if we hope to promote righteousness and be light in a dark world.

Question 29:

WHAT IS A CHRISTIAN'S RESPONSIBILITY CONCERNING MONEY AND WEALTH?

Answer: 1 Timothy 6:17

"Command those who are rich in this present age not to be haughty, nor to trust in uncertain riches but in the living God, who gives us richly all things to enjoy."

Further explanation:

Wealth is a gift from God and should be received with thanksgiving, generosity, and stewardship (1 Timothy 6:17-19; 2 Corinthians 8-9). The Bible offers more than 2,000 verses on the subject of money. It discusses private property, private contracts, caring for the poor, laziness, staying out of debt, not being greedy, working for your food, investing for the future, leaving an inheritance to children, bribery, extortion, profit and loss, serving your customer, and much more. Here is a summary of the basic lessons from the Bible about money:

- Do not set your heart on riches, and especially be on your guard against oppression and robbery (Psalm 62:10; James 5:1-6).

- God calls us to be content with what we have rather than coveting what others have (Exodus 20:17; Hebrews 13:5).

- If we place so much importance on money that we start loving it, we are liable to unleash all kinds of evil and sorrow (Psalm 52:1-7; Matthew 13:22; 1 Timothy 6:6-10; Revelation 3:17).

- Give God praise and thanks for any and all resources that you have, and honor Him by giving freely to others (Deuteronomy 8:11-18; Proverbs 3:9-10; Matthew 10:8; Acts 20:35).

- Building your reputation around money is false; it can lead to dangerous and devastating results, as was the case for one couple in the early church (Acts 5:1-11).

Question 30:

IN WHAT ARE CHRISTIANS TO PLACE THEIR CONFIDENCE?

Answer: Galatians 6:14

"But God forbid that I should boast except in the cross of our Lord Jesus Christ, by whom the world has been crucified to me, and I to the world."

Further explanation:

The Bible tells us to boast only in Christ and the work of the cross and to have confidence in the Lord, not in our own works or abilities apart from Christ (Proverbs 14:26). In 2 Corinthians 12:9 we are told to boast in our weaknesses so the power of Christ may be seen in us.

Those that argue self-love, self-esteem, or having a healthy self-image are Biblical often justify their teaching by using Leviticus 19:18, which Jesus quotes in Luke 10:27—"you shall love your neighbor as yourself." But in the Leviticus passage, God's instructions include a list of ways we should treat other individuals respectfully in our daily conduct. The direction never shifts from social interaction to descriptions of our own inner esteem or affirmation of our goodness.

Self-love in Leviticus and Luke refers to a person's natural inclination to watch out for his or her own welfare. In the physical realm, this simply allows people to survive. It is an instinctive motivation that does not require a lengthy decision-making process.

To teach self-esteem—or its corollary, mankind's basic goodness—is to say that people are not really 100% in need of Jesus Christ and His sacrifice on the cross. It suggests that we are pretty much good enough to face judgment, and perhaps all the cross really did was to shore up our natural human failings, shortcomings, or flaws—not redeem some overwhelming condition like *depravity*.

Question 31:

WHAT IS GOD'S WARNING ABOUT BEING DECEIVED AND CHEATED?

Answer: Colossians 2:8

"Beware lest anyone cheat you through philosophy and empty deceit, according to the tradition of men, according to the basic principles of the world, and not according to Christ."

Further explanation:

Studies show that, before they graduate from college, three-fourths of young people from *Christian* homes end up rejecting the faith they claimed to possess. When you consider the foundation of sand upon which worldviews are often built, it becomes evident why theirs collapses when secular winds and waves of skepticism, criticism, unbelief, and doubt undermine them.

If children and young adults have not built a Biblical worldview verse by verse from the Word of God, then we should not be surprised that most of them eventually walk away from the faith in college. Unlike some of us, writers of Scripture were not in denial on this issue. They warned that drifting from the faith can happen if we do not regularly study the Bible and memorize Scripture.

Question 32:

WHY DID JESUS CHRIST HAVE TO DIE FOR OUR SINS?

Answer: 2 Corinthians 5:21

"For He made Him who knew no sin to be sin for us, that we might become the righteousness of God in Him."

Further explanation:

Dr. Erwin Lutzer, outstanding author, Worldview Weekend speaker, and pastor of Moody Church in Chicago, attended a symposium on world religions in 1994. He walked through the convention center, visiting with some of the 7,000 attendees. He spoke with a Hindu, a Buddhist, a Bahai, and a Muslim, among others, asking them if their teachers or prophets were without sin. Dr. Lutzer describes this experience in his superb book, *Called*:

> Why was I searching for a sinless Savior? Because I don't want to have to trust a Savior who is in the same predicament as I am. I can't trust my eternal soul to someone who is still working through his own imperfections. Since I'm a sinner, I need someone who is standing on higher ground.
>
> Understandably, none of the religious leaders I spoke with even claimed to have a Savior. Their prophets, they said, showed the way, but made no pretense to be able to personally forgive sins or transform so much as a single human being. Like a street sign, they gave directions, but were not able to take us where we need to go. If we need any saving, we will have to do it ourselves.
>
> The reason is obvious: No matter how wise,

no matter how gifted, no matter how influential other prophets, gurus, and teachers might be, they had the presence of mind to know that they were imperfect just like the rest of us. They never even presumed to be able to reach down into the murky water of human depravity and bring sinners into the presence of God.[12]

Question 33:

HOW DOES A BELIEVER LIVE A VICTORIOUS CHRISTIAN LIFE?

Answer: Galatians 2:20

"I have been crucified with Christ; it is no longer I who live, but Christ lives in me; and the life which I now live in the flesh I live by faith in the Son of God, who loved me and gave Himself for me."

Further explanation:

"[K]nowing this, that our old man was crucified with Him, that the body of sin might be done away with, that we should no longer be slaves of sin. For he who has died has been freed from sin" (Romans 6:6-7).

When we place our trust in Jesus Christ as our Lord and Savior, we become new creations. Although we still live in this world and are still tempted to sin, we are no longer slaves to sin but slaves to Christ. Dead to sin and alive in Christ each day, we will experience an ever-greater ability to overcome sin and display the fruits of a true believer.

The Christian who has surrendered his or her life to Christ may be called to reject even the natural impulse for self-preservation and to accept positions that are not safe and comfortable. If the martyrs of Christian history had put the instinct of self-love before their Christian calling, they would not have submitted to premature death. They placed a higher priority on fulfilling the will of God through their lives.

The challenge for the true convert of Christ in today's postmodern world is to recognize and reject the unbiblical version of self-love, as taught by its humanistic and psychological proponents, or even the natural impulse for self-preservation when it conflicts with God's desire for our living out Biblical truth. That may not result in the feel-good version of life, but it matches Jesus' way to achieve an abundant one.

Question 34:

WHERE DOES EVERY GOOD GIFT COME FROM?

Answer: James 1:17

"Every good gift and every perfect gift is from above, and comes down from the Father of lights, with whom there is no variation or shadow of turning."

Further explanation:

God is always the same, He is always good, and He always opposes evil. Moral relativism, on the other hand, is the belief that there is no absolute standard of right or wrong, good or evil. Morals and ethics are autonomous and can evolve to fit the needs and desires of an individual and society. Therefore, moral relativism and situational ethics are false.

God is the source of goodness, and the Bible presents this truth consistently throughout.

Question 35:

WHAT DOES SATAN DESIRE TO DO TO EVERY PERSON?

Answer: 1 Peter 5:8

"Be sober, be vigilant; because your adversary the devil walks about like a roaring lion, seeking whom he may devour."

Further explanation:

An essay entitled *"If I Were the Devil,"* which has been attributed to radio newsman Paul Harvey, reveals just how successful Satan has been at devouring so much in America:

> If I were the devil, I would gain control of the most powerful nation in the world; I would delude their minds into thinking that they had come from man's effort, instead of God's blessings;…

> I would dupe entire states into relying on gambling for their state revenue;…

> I would make it legal to kill unborn babies;

> I would make it socially acceptable to take one's own life, and invent machines to make it convenient;…

> I would take God out of the schools, where even the mention of His name was grounds for a lawsuit;…

> I would get control of the media, so that every night I could pollute the mind of every family member with my agenda;

> I would attack the family, the backbone of any nation

I would make divorce acceptable and easy, even fashionable. If the family crumbles, so does the nation;...

I would convince the world that people are born homosexuals, and that their lifestyles should be accepted;...

I would persuade people that the Church is irrelevant and out of date, and the Bible is for the naive;

I would dull the minds of Christians, and make them believe that prayer is not important, and that faithfulness and obedience are optional;

Hmmm.... I guess if I were the devil, I'd leave things pretty much the way they are.

Question 36:

WHAT DOES THE BIBLE SAY ABOUT ABORTION?

Answer: Exodus 21:22-23

"If men fight, and hurt a woman with child, so that she gives birth prematurely, yet no harm follows, he shall surely be punished accordingly as the woman's husband imposes on him; and he shall pay as the judges determine. But if any harm follows, then you shall give life for life...."

Further explanation:

Psalm 51:5 explains that even a baby has a sin nature. It is also noteworthy that the Biblical Greek word for "baby" is the same whether referring to a child inside or outside of his or her mother, clearly suggesting that God views the born and unborn baby equally. The Biblical worldview argues that abortion is murder, and the Sixth Commandment is clear on that one: "You shall not murder."

Question 37:

WHAT DOES THE BIBLE SAY ABOUT BEING LAZY?

Answer: 2 Thessalonians 3:10

"For even when we were with you, we commanded you this: If anyone will not work, neither shall he eat."

Further explanation:

Americans have spent billions of dollars on welfare programs that subsidize laziness and irresponsibility. For people in need of assistance, the burden should not be placed on the government but on their families and the Church. Nothing in the U.S. Constitution gives the government the right to take money from one group of Americans and give it to another. Unfortunately, now that the federal government has become the cow upon which millions suckle their daily sustenance, we face the monumental problem of how to wean them from government milk and into a life of work, responsibility, productivity, and self-determination.

There is no Biblical justification for providing financial assistance to lazy people. When individuals are forced to accept responsibility by facing the consequences of wrong actions and decisions, they learn not to be irresponsible and lazy. Government intervention also creates a disincentive for those who should be helping solve the problems of legitimately needy people. As more and more people have looked to the government instead of to local churches for crisis assistance, churches have reduced or redirected their benevolent funds and programs and are thus missing out on potential opportunities for ministry.

Jesus tells us that the poor will always be with us.

The reason is that people's sins often lead them into poverty. A Biblical definition is someone that does not have clothing, food, or shelter, or sometimes it is a reference to a person's spiritual, not financial, condition.

Question 38:

WHAT DOES THE BIBLE SAY ABOUT GAMBLING?

Answer: Proverbs 11:18

"The wicked man does deceptive work, but he who sows righteousness will have a sure reward."

Further explanation:

As noted earlier, Romans 13:1-4 says the purpose of civil government is to protect the righteous and punish the wicked. But states that sponsor gambling are encouraging a vice that God says to avoid. Gambling encourages laziness, greed, and covetousness, and it takes advantage of the poor.

Exodus 20:17 says we are not to covet that which belongs to others, but when people gamble, they are coveting that which is not rightfully theirs and which they have not earned through work or investing. We are to put our hands "to the plow" and *earn* money through hard work, not by pursuing get-rich-quick schemes or ill-gotten gains.

State-sponsored gambling is wrong because gambling is by its very nature deceptive in its marketing tactics. The commercials promise a great time, lots of fun and happiness, and imply that a gambler will get rich. This is outright deception, which the Bible condemns.

National studies reveal that people who pay the dearest price for the vice of gambling are those in low-income families. Many low-income people who play the lottery are misappropriating money that should be used for food, housing, healthcare, clothes, and other basics of life. First Timothy 5:8 is clear on just how wrong this is: "But if anyone does not provide for his own, and especially for those of his household, he has denied the faith and is worse than an unbeliever" (1 Timothy 5:8).

Question 39:

WHAT DOES THE BIBLE SAY ABOUT ACTIVE EUTHANASIA?

Answer: Matthew 5:21

"You have heard that it was said to those of old, 'You shall not murder, and whoever murders will be in danger of the judgment.'"

Further explanation:

Kerby Anderson describes the consequences of legalizing active euthanasia:

> First, physician-assisted suicide would change the nature of the medical profession itself. Physicians would be cast in the role of killers rather than healers. The Hippocratic Oath was written to place the medical profession on the foundation of healing, not killing. For twenty-four hundred years patients have had the assurance that doctors have taken an oath to heal them, not kill them. This would change with legalized euthanasia.

> Second, medical care would be affected. Physicians would begin to ration healthcare so that elderly and severely disabled patients would not be receiving the same quality of care as everyone else.

> Legalizing euthanasia would result in less care for the dying, rather than better care. Legalizing physician-assisted suicide would open the door to anyone wanting the "right" to kill themselves. Soon this would apply not only to voluntary euthanasia but also to involuntary euthanasia as various court precedents began to broaden the application of the right to die to other groups in society, like the disabled or the clinically depressed.[13]

The Biblical position on "euthanasia," or taking a life, is absolute. The death of King Saul is an important example of verses that focus on the sin taking a person's life (2 Samuel 1:1-16). "In whose hand is the life of every living thing, and the breath of all mankind?" (Job 12:10). This verse makes it clear that man is not to intervene and end the life of anyone except for capital punishment and self-defense.

Question 40:

WHAT SHOULD CHRISTIANS DO WHEN THEY HAVE PROBLEMS OR EXPERIENCE ANXIETY?

Answer: Philippians 4:6-7

"Be anxious for nothing, but in everything by prayer and supplication, with thanksgiving, let your requests be made known to God; and the peace of God, which surpasses all understanding, will guard your hearts and minds through Christ Jesus."

Further explanation:

The Bible tells us that it is a sin to worry and fret. When we do, we are not trusting the Lord. For many people, their fears and worries become so great that they experience anxiety. Millions of Americans now take pills for anxiety. The Bible tells us that we don't have to be anxious or experience anxiety if we will trust the Lord and cast our cares on Him.

Anxiety can be caused from unconfessed sin in our lives. In Psalm 38:4-6 we see that King David was experiencing deep anxiety for the sin in his life: "For my iniquities have gone over my head; like a heavy burden they are too heavy for me. My wounds are foul and festering because of my foolishness. I am troubled, I am bowed down greatly; I go mourning all the day long."

In Psalm 32:5, King David tells us what happened when he confessed his sin to the Lord: "I acknowledged my sin to You, and my iniquity I have not hidden. I said, 'I will confess my transgressions to the Lord,' and You forgave the iniquity of my sin."

In Psalm 139:23-24 King David pleads to the Lord to convict him of any sin in his life that is causing him to be anxious: "Search me, O God, and know my heart; try me, and know my anxieties; and see if there is any wicked way in me, and lead me in the way everlasting."

Question 41:

WHAT IS THE DIFFERENCE BETWEEN SOMEONE WHO GAINS WEALTH OVER TIME THROUGH HARD WORK AND THE PERSON WHO STRIVES TO GET RICH QUICKLY?

Answer: Proverbs 28:20

"A faithful man will abound with blessings, but he who hastens to get rich will not go unpunished."

Further explanation:

Proverbs 12:11 notes that "He who tills his land will be satisfied with bread, but he who follows frivolity is devoid of understanding." Proverbs 28:20 observes, "A faithful man will abound with blessings, but he who hastens to get rich will not go unpunished."

The New Testament picks up the theme: "Command those who are rich in this present age not to be haughty, nor to trust in uncertain riches but in the living God, who gives us richly all things to enjoy" (1 Timothy 6:17). If we place so much importance on money that we start loving it, we are liable to unleash all kinds of evil and sorrow (Psalm 52:1-7; Matthew 13:22; 1 Timothy 6:6-10; Revelation 3:17). We are warned not to set our hearts on riches, and especially to be on our guard against oppression and robbery (Ps. 62:10; James 5:1-6

The Bible never says that money is the root of all evil, but that the *love* of money is a root of all kinds of evil (1 Timothy 6:10). The Bible tells us: to obtain wealth over the course of time through the sweat of our brows, to use our wealth to be a blessing to others, to provide for our families and those in need, to further the proclamation of the gospel of Jesus Christ, and to gain friends and influence for accomplishing Godly objectives.

Question 42:

WHAT SHOULD BE THE STANDARD FOR OUR THOUGHT LIFE AND ENTERTAINMENT?

Answer: Philippians 4:8

"Finally, brethren, whatever things are true, whatever things are noble, whatever things are just, whatever things are pure, whatever things are lovely, whatever things are of good report, if there is any virtue and if there is anything praiseworthy—meditate on these things."

Further explanation:

I know of families who have placed this verse on top of their television and use it as a reminder to choose wisely the television programs and DVDs they view. This verse should also be our standard when we listen to music, play a video game, or surf the internet.

There are at least two reasons why we need to be careful about what entertainment we choose:

(1) Everything we do should bring honor and glory to God. 1 Corinthians 10:31 says, "Therefore, whether you eat or drink, or whatever you do, do all to the glory of God."

(2) What we view impacts our thinking, and our thinking impacts who we are and what we do. Proverbs 23:7 says, "For as he thinks in his heart, so is he."

Our thought life is critical to who we are and what we do, and this is why it is so important to commit God's Word to memory. When we ponder the Scriptures we have memorized, they will assist us to live a life that brings honor and glory to God.

Question 43:

WHAT DID JESUS SAY WAS THE FIRST AND GREAT COMMANDMENT?

Answer: Matthew 22:37

"Jesus said to him,
'You shall love the Lord your God
with all your heart, with all your soul,
and with all your mind.'

This is the first and great commandment."

Further explanation:

This verse originally appears in Deuteronomy 6:5 as a part of the *Shema*. In Deuteronomy 6:4-12 God gives Israel a strategy for the spiritual lives of their families as they prepare to enter the promised land. It begins with the Hebrew word "Shema'" which in English means "hear:" "Hear, O Israel: The Lord our God, the Lord is one!" (Deuteronomy 6:4).

Once God gets their attention, He continues: "You shall love the Lord your God with all your heart, with all your soul, and with all your strength."

My friend and Worldview Weekend speaker and columnist Marshall Foster notes that the Shema lays out four specific ways the children of Israel are to accomplish the goal of loving and serving God:

- know God and His character and attributes;
- love the Lord through a personal relationship and faith;
- teach God's truth to your children; and
- mark yourself, your home, and your business with obedience to God's law.[14]

The children of Israel not only committed the Scriptures to memory but literally wrote them on the doorposts and gates of their homes. God's command to do these things reveals how important it is to the Lord that we memorize Scripture, as you are doing with the assistance of this book. The Lord is pleased with your commitment to memorize His Word. It reveals your desire to love the Lord Your God with all your heart, soul, strength, and mind.

Question 44:

WHAT DID PETER SAY ABOUT JESUS CHRIST AFTER LIVING WITH HIM FOR THREE YEARS?

Answer: 1 Peter 2:22

"Who committed no sin, or was deceit found in His mouth."

Further explanation:

Peter spent three years with Jesus Christ as one of His disciples. Peter saw Jesus during His public moments and private moments and declared that never, not even one time, did he ever see Jesus say or do anything deceitful.

Peter was not the only one could find nothing wrong in Jesus. When He was presented to Pilate for trial prior to His crucifixion, Pilate declared to the chief priests and hostile crowd, "I find no fault in this Man" (Luke 23:4).

Remember, too, skeptics and critics spent a great deal of time listening to what Jesus said in hopes of catching Him in a sin, and, yet, they could not attribute even one wrongdoing to Jesus.

Jesus even asked His enemies to name even one sin that He had committed: "Which of you convicts Me of sin?" (John 8:46) His critics were silent.

Jesus Christ was able to save us because He was and is the sinless Savior.

Question 45:

HOW CAN A CHRISTIAN OBTAIN GREAT GAIN?

Answer: 1 Timothy 6:6

"Now godliness with contentment is great gain."

Further explanation:

Psalm 37:16 puts it this way: "A little that a righteous man has is better than the riches of many wicked." Proverbs 16:8 gives us this admonishment: "Better is a little with righteousness, than vast revenues without justice."

When George Beverly Shea was 23 years old, he was offered a contract with a recording company that would have made him very wealthy. But George was convicted that his voice should be used only for singing songs that proclaim the gospel of Jesus Christ. He found a poem called *I'd Rather Have Jesus* by Rhea Miller and sat down at the family piano to put the poem to music. For his 80-plus years Mr. Shea has used his voice to sing only Christian hymns in churches, crusades, and Christian meetings, and this song has become a treasured classic for millions of Christians throughout the world. As you read the words, think about a 23-year-old George struggling with a choice between a full-time music ministry or a lucrative singing career.

I'd rather have Jesus than silver or gold;
     I'd rather be His than have riches untold;
I'd rather have Jesus than houses or lands.
     I'd rather be led by His nail-pierced hand.
I'd rather have Jesus than men's applause;
     I'd rather be faithful to His dear cause;

I'd rather have Jesus than world-wide fame.
> I'd rather be true to His holy name.

(Chorus) Than to be the king of a vast domain
> or be held in sin's dread sway.

I'd rather have Jesus than anything
> this world affords today.

Question 46:

WHO ARE CHRISTIANS TO IMITATE OR LOOK TO AS THEIR ROLE MODEL?

Answer: Ephesians 5:1

"Therefore be imitators of God as dear children."

Further explanation:

The news media reports the lives and shenanigans of actors, actresses, politicians, and athletes as though everything they do is important, interesting, and noteworthy. Almost every national television news program has become a video tabloid.

But the reason the media cover the lives of celebrities as they do is that it draws a large audience. American children, teens, and adults seek to imitate today's pop culture and its icons rather than Christ.

Ephesians 5:1 makes clear that our goal should be to imitate Jesus Christ, not pop-culture icons.

Not one author, businessman, president, congressman, general, talk-show host, actor, or athlete has ever accomplished—even by earthly standards—that which was accomplished by Jesus Christ. As historian Philip Schaff puts it, "Born in a manager and crucified as a malefactor, He now controls the destinies of the civilized world and rules a spiritual empire which embraces one-third of the inhabitants of the globe."[15]

In Luke 9:23 Jesus tells us how His followers should imitate Him: "Then He said to them, 'If anyone desires to come after Me, let him deny himself, and take up his cross daily, and follow Me.'"

To pick up your cross means to deny yourself or to deny your own desires in deference to the will of God.

Question 47:

WHAT SEVEN THINGS DOES THE LORD HATE?

Answer: Proverbs 6:16-19

"These six things the Lord hates, yes, seven are an abomination to Him: a proud look, a lying tongue, hands that shed innocent blood, a heart that devises wicked plans, feet that are swift in running to evil, a false witness who speaks lies, and one who sows discord among brethren."

Further explanation:

In the majority of America's churches, we rarely hear that God *hates*, but He does. Many pastors refuse to preach anything but what God loves. God is love, and God so loved the world that He sent His Son Jesus Christ to save us from our sins. However, the love of God has no context if we don't also teach about the wrath of God and the judgment to come.

Did you know, for instance, that the Bible mentions hell more often then it does heaven? Because God is righteous and just, He must judge the sins of the world, and when self-professing Christians are purposefully silent on what God hates in order to be politically correct, I can tell you that God hates it, because He hates a lying tongue and a false witness.

Question 48:

WHY SHOULD WE NOT BE SURPRISED OR DETERRED WHEN THE WORLD MAKES FUN OF OUR WORLDVIEW AND FAITH IN JESUS CHRIST?

Answer: 1 Corinthians 1:18

"For the message of the cross is foolishness to those who are perishing, but to us who are being saved it is the power of God."

Further explanation:

Many skeptics and critics of Christianity have been presented truth in a loving way, are drawn by the Holy Spirit, become Christians, and then become great defenders of the faith. The apostle Paul is a well-known example. But while some are converted, many are not. In fact, Romans 1:18 tells us that many will *suppress* the truth. They reject their own consciences and knowingly and willingly continue in their sin.

Despite understanding who God is, many reject Him, refuse to pursue Him, suppress the truth, and then become futile and foolish in their thinking (Romans 1:20-21). And then when they encounter Christians and the truth of Christianity, they can have a visceral reaction, rejecting what they hear and, at times, verbally attacking and ridiculing Christians.

Romans 1:22 says, "Professing to be wise, they became fools." But the world says Christians are ignorant, naive, silly, and uneducated because we have faith in that which is unseen. Yet, the Bible says that those whom the world says are the really smart folks become fools because they reject what should be obvious—that there is an all-powerful, all-knowing God who will judge the world in righteousness.

Question 49:

HOW SHOULD CHRISTIANS LIVE?

Answer: Philippians 1:27-28

"Only let your conduct be worthy of the gospel of Christ, so that whether I come and see you or am absent, I may hear of your affairs, that you stand fast in one spirit, with one mind striving together for the faith of the gospel, and not in any way terrified by your adversaries...."

Further explanation:

As Christians we should live out our faith in all areas of life, having a Biblical worldview and proclaiming the gospel, the truth of God's Word, and its practical application for daily living. Christians must be aware of the worldviews that compete for allegiance.

First Chronicles 12:32 says that the sons of Issachar were called wise because they understood the times and knew what God would have them to do. This should be an example to us to understand the times in which we live, to know how a Biblical worldview applies, and to understand the worldviews that compete with Christianity.

Cosmic Humanism (New Age) believes in pantheism, the belief that God is in everything. It (not He) is a force you can use to your advantage through the power of your mind. Secular Humanism believes there is no God, that people are the highest order of being and therefore not accountable to God. Christians believe mankind is born with a sin nature but that each person has a free will and can choose to be a slave to sin or a servant of Jesus Christ.

A person worldview impacts every area of his or her life. As a Christian, you are to love the Lord your God with all your heart, soul, strength, and mind, and it is your responsibility to sharpen your mind to think and live according to a Christian worldview.

Question 50:

APART FROM SALVATION THROUGH JESUS CHRIST, WHAT IS THE END RESULT OF OUR SIN?

Answer: Romans 6:23

"For the wages of sin is death, but the gift of God is eternal life in Christ Jesus our Lord."

Further explanation:

This verse promises two things:

- that sin brings death, and
- that eternal life is guaranteed through JesusChrist.

These two promises are seen throughout Scripture. The Bible promises death and judgment for unrepentant sinners and promises salvation, eternal life, and the hope of glory for those who repent and place their faith in Jesus Christ.

For the believer who has repented of his sins and placed his faith in Jesus Christ, his sins are not counted against him. Psalm 103:11-12 says, "For as the heavens are high above the earth, so great is His mercy toward those who fear Him; as far as the east is from the west, so far has He removed our transgressions from us."

John 3:36 puts it this way: "He who believes in the Son has everlasting life; and he who does not believe the Son shall not see life, but the wrath of God abides on him." John 3:16 explains that those who do not place their faith and trust in Jesus Christ will perish.

Hebrews 9:27 also promises that you don't get a second chance after death, but that it is appointed unto every man to die and then face judgment. Second Corinthians 13:5 puts it this way: "Examine yourselves as to whether you are in the faith. Test yourselves. Do you not know yourselves, that Jesus Christ is in you?—unless indeed you are disqualified."

Question 51:

WHAT DOES GOD DESIRE FOR THE WICKED?

Answer: Ezekiel 33:11

"Say to them:
'As I live,' says the Lord God,
'I have no pleasure in the death
of the wicked, but that the wicked turn
from his way and live.'"

Further explanation:

Second Peter 3:9 further states the Lord's desire for all people: "The Lord is not slack concerning His promise, as some count slackness, but is longsuffering toward us, not willing that any should perish but that all should come to repentance."

The Lord does not want anyone to perish or spend eternity in hell, but He also maintains that repentance is key to salvation. There is no salvation without repentance. Grace is extended only to those who repent.

This verse also reveals God's patience. God could end the life of the unbeliever at anytime and would be completely justified in doing so. However, He has again and again withheld judgment on unbelievers so His Holy Spirit might convict and draw them to repentance and salvation. Each and every Christian has been the recipient of God's patience. It was God's patience that preserved them until their day of salvation, because God is not willing that any should perish but that all should come to repentance.

The essence and message of 2 Peter 3:9 is repeated in Romans 2:4: "Or do you despise the riches of His goodness, forbearance, and longsuffering, not knowing that the goodness of God leads you to repentance?"

The psalmist puts it this way in Psalm 86:15: "But You, O Lord, are a God full of compassion, and gracious, longsuffering and abundant in mercy and truth."

Question 52:

WHAT ARE WE TO DO WITH EVERY THOUGHT?

Answer: 2 Corinthians 10:5

"Casting down arguments and every high thing that exalts itself against the knowledge of God, bringing every thought into captivity to the obedience of Christ."

Further explanation:

This verse calls for Christians to be ready to destroy, cast down, refute and expose as false every argument, idea, or belief that is contrary to the character and nature of God. It calls us to be involved in apologetics—the defense of the essential doctrines of Christianity.

It is crucial that we destroy every argument raised up against the knowledge of God without destroying the people who raise them. Jesus commanded the twelve to be "wise as serpents and harmless as doves" (Matthew 10:16).

In Jude 3 we are exhorted to "contend earnestly for the faith." While we are to be loving in our defense of the gospel, that does not mean we should be weak or timid. The most loving thing we can do for those who are lost is to tell them they are wrong so they can repent of their sins and avoid God's wrath.

Everything we read, look at and think needs to be seen through a Biblical grid to determine if it is in agreement with the character and nature of God. If a thought is not consistent with God's character and nature, then it needs to be brought into captivity or arrested so that it surrenders, gives up, or even retreats. That way, our minds and thoughts are pleasing to God.

NOTES

[1] S.C. Meyer, "The Methodological Equivalence of Design and Descent: Can There Be a 'Scientific Theory of Creation?'" *The Creation Hypothesis*, by S.C. Meyer (Downers Grove, IL: Intervarsity Press, 1994), p. 98,

[2] William Paley, *Evidence of Christianity* (London: 1851), p.26.

[3] Ibid., p.26.

[4] "Drug Prevention Curricula" U.S. Department of Education, 1988

[5] Ray Comfort keynote presentation: *Hell's Best Kept Secret* www.livingwaters.com

[6] Mark Cahill, *One Thing You Can't Do in Heaven*, (Mark Cahill. org: 2002) p.131.

[7] Josh McDowell and Bob Hostetler, *Beyond Belief to Convictions* (Wheaton: Tyndale House, 2002), p.54.

[8] Ibid. p. 54

[9] Tim LaHaye, *Jesus Who is He?* (Multnomah Books, Sister, Oregon, 1996) pp.265

[10] Anderson, *Moral Dilemmas,* p. 223-224

[11] Dr. D. James Kennedy, *Lord of All: Developing A Christian World-and-Life View* (Wheaton, IL: Crossway, 2005), 130.

[12] Erwin Lutzer, *Christ Among Other Gods* (Chicago: Moody Press, 1994), p. 62-64.

[13] Anderson, *Moral Dilemmas,* p.27-28

[14] Marshall Foster, *No Retreats, No Reserves, No Regrets*, (Stewart House Press, St. Paul, MN, 2000) p. 7-8.

[15] Philip Schaff, *The Person of Christ* (New York: Doran, 1913) 137-138.

ABOUT THE AUTHOR

Brannon Howse is president and founder of American Family Policy Institute and Worldview Weekend, America's largest Christian worldview conference series. Founded in 1993, Worldview Weekend is now held in seventeen states each year with an annual attendance of approximately 20,000. Brannon is also:

- Founder of www.christianworldviewnetwork.com, which features columns and articles by some of America's best Christian worldview authors and speakers.

- Founder of Worldview Weekend Online Institute (www.worldviewtraining.com), a 12-week online course exploring the Biblical worldview. The course is also available as in-class curriculum featuring leader and student manuals, DVDs, CDs, and tests.

- Brannon served as the literary agent for Michael Reagan, son of President Reagan, for his book Twice Adopted which was released in October of 2004.

- Host of the Worldview Weekend Family Reunion held in Branson, Missouri, each spring and attended by more than 2,000 people. The three-day event features nationally known speakers, comedians, and musicians.

- Brannon has served as the education reporter for *The Michael Reagan* show since 1993 and serves as a frequent guest host. Brannon was honored to sit in and host Mike's national radio show during the week that Mike was attending his father's funeral and memorial services.

- Brannon is the author of eight books on education, civil government, public policy, family issues, and Christian worldview topics.

- President of Worldview Weekend Publishing.

- Co-host of *Christian Worldview This Week*, a weekly radio broadcast heard on more than 225 stations each week.

- Has apppeared on over 600 radio and television programs, including *The O'Reilly Factor* (Fox News), *The News on MSNBC*, *Truths That Transform with Dr. D. James Kennedy*, *The G. Gordon Liddy Show*, *The Michael Reagan Show*, *The Ken Hamblin Show*, *The Oliver North Show*, *Action Sixties*, *Point of View*, *Family News and Focus*, *U.S.A. Radio News*, and *Standard News*.

About Worldview
Weekend Conferences

Christians today are bombarded with information and opinions by the media, schools, and government. No one can hope to assimilate the avalanche of data. So who could possibly understand the times in which we live? Not many! But those men and women who do become the next generation of leaders.

The Bible speaks of a small tribe in Israel that "had understanding of the times" and knew "what Israel ought to do," and, as a result, they became leaders (1 Chronicles 12:32). God expects His people to seek earnestly for the truth, rewarding with greater responsibility those who comprehend. Worldview Weekend Conferences are dedicated to teaching you how to understand our times and grasp the opportunity that will give you for leadership.

Worldview Weekend features nationally known speakers such as Josh McDowell, David Limbaugh, David Barton, Kirk Cameron, David Jeremiah, Kerby Anderson, Star Parker, Al Denson, Erwin Lutzer, and others. U.S. Congressman Tom DeLay has been a keynote speaker at Worldview Weekend, as well as the Honorable Dick Armey when he was U.S. House Majority Leader.

To find out more about how to attend the Worldview Weekend of your choice, go to www.worldviewweekend.com.

WORLDVIEW
WEEKEND RESOURCES

We invite you to take advantage of these helpful
Worldview Weekend Resources:

- Visit worldviewweekend.com and check out the **Berean Club**.
  You can load more than 125 Worldview Weekend keynote
  presentations onto your ipod, listen online or burn a cd.

- Further your worldview knowledge by taking our online
  course, **Developing a Christian Worldview.** Try our free demo
  at worldviewtraining.com

- We have DVDs featuring *Kirk Cameron, Ray Comfort, David Barton,
  Josh McDowell, Sean McDowell* and others. Check out our books
  and DVDs in our bookstore at worldviewweekend.com

- Visit christianworldviewnetwork.com for daily news and
  columns from a Biblical worldview perspective.

- Brannon's book, ***One Nation Under Man? The Worldview War
  Between Christians and the Secular Left,*** can be purchased
  from our online bookstore at worldviewweekend.com.